T0129729

LIVING
MOVEMENTS

Movements to Rebalance the Body

PENNY COOPER

BALBOA.
PRESS

A DIVISION OF HAY HOUSE

Balboa Press books may be ordered through booksellers or by contacting:

Balboa Press
A Division of Hay House
1663 Liberty Drive
Bloomington, IN 47403
www.balboapress.com
1 (877) 407-4847

Because of the dynamic nature of the Internet, any web addresses or links contained in this book may have changed since publication and may no longer be valid. The views expressed in this work are solely those of the author and do not necessarily reflect the views of the publisher, and the publisher hereby disclaims any responsibility for them.

The author of this book does not dispense medical advice or prescribe the use of any technique as a form of treatment for physical, emotional, or medical problems without the advice of a physician, either directly or indirectly. The intent of the author is only to offer information of a general nature to help you in your quest for emotional and spiritual well-being. In the event you use any of the information in this book for yourself, which is your constitutional right, the author and the publisher assume no responsibility for your actions.

Any people depicted in stock imagery provided by Getty Images are models, and such images are being used for illustrative purposes only. Certain stock imagery © Getty Images.

Print information available on the last page.

ISBN: 978-1-9822-0004-6 (sc)
ISBN: 978-1-9822-0003-9 (e)

Balboa Press rev. date: 04/20/2018

LIVING
MOVEMENTS

Movements to Rebalance the Body

PENNY COOPER

BALBOA.
PRESS
A DIVISION OF HAY HOUSE

Balboa Press books may be ordered through booksellers or by contacting:

Balboa Press
A Division of Hay House
1663 Liberty Drive
Bloomington, IN 47403
www.balboapress.com
1 (877) 407-4847

Because of the dynamic nature of the Internet, any web addresses or
links contained in this book may have changed since publication and
may no longer be valid. The views expressed in this work are solely those
of the author and do not necessarily reflect the views of the publisher,
and the publisher hereby disclaims any responsibility for them.

The author of this book does not dispense medical advice or prescribe the use
of any technique as a form of treatment for physical, emotional, or medical
problems without the advice of a physician, either directly or indirectly. The
intent of the author is only to offer information of a general nature to help
you in your quest for emotional and spiritual well-being. In the event you use
any of the information in this book for yourself, which is your constitutional
right, the author and the publisher assume no responsibility for your actions.

Any people depicted in stock imagery provided by Getty Images are
models, and such images are being used for illustrative purposes only.
Certain stock imagery © Getty Images.

Print information available on the last page.

ISBN: 978-1-9822-0004-6 (sc)
ISBN: 978-1-9822-0003-9 (e)

Balboa Press rev. date: 04/20/2018

Dedication

To Bonnie.
I feel so blessed to have you in my life.

Contents

Acknowledgements

I would like to thank Sonia Moriceau who helped me find my spiritual side whilst teaching me Healing Shiatsu. To my mother, who always encouraged me to follow my dreams and to do what made me happy. To Rosslyn Galpin for helping me continue on my spiritual journey and being instrumental in guiding me to realise my dreams. My friends, who have supported me without judgement, including: Angela and Paul Richards, Marina Brett, Pam and Oliver Bailey, Lesley and Roy Govier and Tania Kromoloff. A special mention goes to Gillian Haines, who is not only a dear friend and confidante but who drew my beautiful Element Flower. To my daughter Bonnie, who has travelled through this book-writing journey with me, helping with the editing and taking the photos. To Declan Winterton, for his time, patience and camera, in taking the photos with Bonnie.

Blessings

Penny Cooper

Preface

This book came about because I realised, when speaking to other people, that I had to share my journey from stress, depression, anxiety and fatigue to the joyous, healthy life I have now. I knew that if I could achieve this by following a simple set of stretches and doing them whenever and wherever it suited me then anyone could.

By following the set of six simple stretches, you will learn how it can improve your quality of life. You'll feel calmer and more in control, creating less stress physically and emotionally. Your mobility will increase, bringing about increased range of movement.

After suffering a neck and back injury from three car accidents in one year, my mobility was limited; I became depressed, had no energy and lacked any enthusiasm for life. The stress this caused me and my family was becoming irreparable. I realised that if I did not take control of my life I would be stuck, in pain, relying on friends and family to help me, unable to hold a job down, and being miserable. At this point in my life, I had nothing to lose.

So using the skills as a dancer, dance instructor, Shiatsu Practitioner, and massage therapist, I discovered that by doing these simple stretches every day, I gradually increased my mobility and with that, decreased my pain. I felt calmer, happier and more in control of my life. You can read a fuller version of my story by going to: www. releaseyourstress.com.au

To make sure I could help as many people as possible, I used my family and friends as willing guinea pigs to try the movements. I quickly learned that the one set of stretches did not suit everyone. Some of them found it difficult to get into certain positions, due to physical limitations. I researched alternative stretches that still achieved the same result, but in a gentler fashion. Then I went even further to include as many variations as possible for each stretch.

This book has taken many years to put together as I really wanted to make sure my explanations of how to do each stretch was clear.

I also wanted to include an explanation of each of the elements that these stretches originate from. I have included a Question and Answer section to cover some of the most common concerns, but am happy to answer any question that has not been covered by contacting me at: penny@ releaseyourstress.com.au

The book has been divided into four sections and has been designed so that you don't necessarily have to read it in order but can go to any section you want. The first section covers the Questions and Answers. The second section describes the characteristics of each element that is associated with a stretch. The third section shows the movements with photos and a full explanation. The fourth section is a bonus section of some additional movements. So you can jump straight to the movements section if you want and read the rest at a later time.

Blessings,

Penny Cooper

Introduction

My Story

My story goes back to the UK, when I was four years old and I begged my mum to let me join my sister's ballet class. After a lot of mischief-making on my behalf, she finally agreed (actually, the teacher asked her to, as I had a tendency to play up behind her back and make the other students laugh).

This started me on the path of so many different forms of Movement, such as ballet, tap, jazz, modern, ballroom, Latin, rock and roll, aerobics, step, yoga, and others.

I worked as a professional dancer for a few years until, one day, whilst sitting at the hairdressers, I read an article about Shiatsu. It was like something just clicked into place; I had been looking for something more spiritual, that also used Movement, and there it was. I immediately signed up for the four-year course, and loved every minute of it.

My love of learning continued by becoming qualified as a Sports Massage therapist and a dance teacher. I started a business where I would do massage and Shiatsu during the day and teach dance to adults in the evening. Life was going so well.

I came to Australia in January 1995, having been invited by a lovely woman I met at a festival. Whilst on my travels, I met my future husband (although I didn't know it at the time). We travelled together on his motorbike from the southern tip of Melbourne to Cook Town, stopping where and when we wanted. It was on this journey that our beautiful daughter was created.

We settled in Brisbane, where I put most of my attention into raising my beautiful daughter, practicing Shiatsu when I could. I absolutely loved being a mother, and still do. The lessons I have learnt on this journey have been so precious. Although the marriage didn't last, my daughter continues to see her father and they have a very strong bond, something I am truly grateful for.

As a single mum, I decided to get qualified as a teacher so I could share the school holidays with my daughter. This meant I really had no time for anything else, so my Shiatsu and massage business took a step back.

Life started getting stressful, with study, school runs, paying bills, being a mum, trying to make ends meet, and missing my family back in the UK.

It was during this time that my mum passed away. I remember going into my bank and shouting to the teller that they had to lend me money for my daughter and I to go to my mother's funeral. The bank manager came out and, to his credit, immediately organized a credit card for me to pay for the flight. I will be forever grateful to him.

By the time we returned, I was drained. I found I had no motivation or joy left, except for my daughter, and she kept me going as only a young child can – thank goodness.

In 2007, my daughter and I were driving home from her school disco when a car crossed over the road in front of me. It was a major impact, with both of us needing hospital treatment. This was followed by two more car accidents in the same year. None of them were my doing, but left me with neck damage, a sore back, headaches, depression, and stress.

By this time, I was feeling isolated, lonely, worthless and deeply depressed. I was at my lowest ebb. I was unfit, putting on weight and really didn't like myself.

The turning point came when I spotted a small advert in the local paper promoting dance classes for older women. The thought of being able to dance brought a huge smile to my face, and I remember thinking to myself that I needed to go, whatever it took. I remember how scared I was of going to my first class, but I was determined to turn my life around.

Dancing again made me so happy, but the pain in my back and neck was not so great. I remembered my earlier training in Shiatsu and dance, and realized that I already had all the tools I needed to help myself.

Slowly, I started doing these stretches and, although a bit tender and somewhat restrictive to begin with, it wasn't too long before my mobility increased – as did my energy and mood. I had found a way to not only manage my neck and back pain, but also release my stress with it.

In 2013, I completed the QSCA (Quantum Success Coaching Academy) Life Coach course, learning how to let go of the emotional stress attached to my situation and now practice as a Qualified Stress Release Life Coach, as well as holding weekly fitness and meditation classes.

I love my life and everything about it. I am so grateful for seeing that one small ad that led me on this journey to self-love.

Blessings,

Penny Cooper

About Meridian Movements

Questions and Answers

When learning anything new, there are so many questions you want answered. To that end, I have tried to answer as many questions as I could think of, with the help of friends and family, that may come up for you before you start. Some of these Q-and-As may seem like just plain common sense, but I felt that I should cover everything, as there will be those who have never done these types of Movements before, while for others it will be more familiar.

If you are of the latter group, please feel free to skip to the exercises. However, you can always refer back to this chapter if you need to.

What are 'Meridian Movements'?

Meridian Movements are a sequence of gentle stretches that open up the Meridian lines in the body to promote well-being.

Meridians are found all through the body, as the following diagram shows.

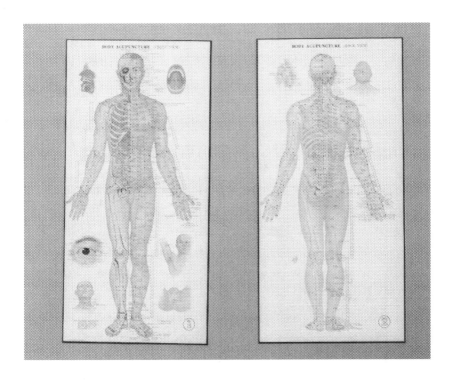

Human Body Meridians

Why Would I Do Meridian Movements?

By doing Meridian Movements, you will find it calms the mind, relieves stress and fatigue and relaxes your muscles and joints, bringing a wonderful sense of peace and relaxation.

The calmer and more relaxed you become, the less stress you will put on yourself and, therefore, your body.

When there is less stress put on your body, symptoms like hypertension, gastric ulcers, insomnia, indigestion and constipation can start improving.

It can help emotional symptoms, too, such as depression, lethargy and/or mental fatigue, as often these can be triggered by any or all of the above symptoms.

To use an old analogy, it is like peeling the proverbial onion. If each layer is seen in terms of a physical distress (an energy blockage), by continually peeling these layers off you will find that, by the time you get to the core, those emotional symptoms have greatly reduced and, in some cases, disappeared altogether.

This is because behind nearly all the physical distress is an emotional distress that preceded it. When these emotions are not dealt with, either consciously or unconsciously, the body tries to give you a warning signal and this can manifest as aches and pains. As time goes by and more emotions get left unexamined, these discomforts you are experiencing increase.

I look at it as layers of distress piling on top of one another; as they do this, your body gets worn out trying to deal with it all, until the time comes when you start physically and emotionally shutting down. This, to me, is when you start experiencing lethargy, fatigue, and depression in a big way.

It never 'just happens'—that, one day, you are feeling great and the next you feel totally exhausted and depressed. It is a gradual process, sometimes taking many years to build up. However, even if you have been feeling exhausted and depressed for a long time, you will still have good days and bad days.

The body is an amazing piece of machinery and, even when you are at your lowest point, you can often find it within you to laugh and carry on as if you haven't a care in the world. This is our protective mechanism. Even so, we all have a breaking point.

The best way to prevent this from happening is to look after yourself. By including the Meridian Movements in your daily routine, you can slowly rid yourself of all those distresses/blockages and maintain the sort of life you see other people having and always wanted for yourself.

Who Can Do Meridian Movements?

Most people of any age can have a go at these Movements and, as I will explain later, there are various techniques you can use to compensate for any lack of mobility or flexibility you may have.

Let me say right away that you do not have to be super fit or super flexible to do these Movements. In fact, although you may find your flexibility increases as you do these Movements, you should only view this as an added bonus and not the sole purpose of the Meridian Movements.

As long as you go at your own pace, moving into the various positions as shown without over stretching yourself and ignoring what your body is telling you, you should find these Meridian Movements extremely beneficial.

Where Can I Do Meridian Movements?

This very much comes down to your personal choice. It can depend on where you live or how much space you have in your home. If you live in a hot climate, you may consider doing these Meridian Movements outside for part or all of the year. However, if you live in a colder climate then that may not be an option.

As a lot of these Movements are done on the floor, you will need to find an area that allows you enough space to lie down comfortably with a bit of room to either side of you.

What Do I Do The Meridian Movements On?

Over the years, I have used my Shiatsu mat, a camping mat, a doona (duvet), the carpet (with and without a towel), the grass (with and without a towel), a sheepskin rug, folded blankets, and just a towel. At certain times in my life, I have had to rely on my imagination and use anything I could get my hands on.

Generally, though, the best item to use is a yoga/ exercise mat with or without a towel over it. These are easy to find and quite cheap to purchase, plus they can be rolled up and put away easily.

If you are planning on just using the floor or carpet, you might want to put a towel or blanket down for some extra cushioning for your ankles as they can dig into the floor during some of the positions. You can use extra towels or something similar if you need to.

If you are planning on going outside to perform these Meridian Movements, just make sure that you have enough cushioning underneath you, especially if you are on a hard surface like concrete. Do make sure you are careful in the hotter climates and wear sun protection.

It is up to you to decide what and where is best for you; there is nothing wrong with trying out different places, surfaces and equipment, just as long as you are comfortable.

What Do I Wear For Meridian Movements?

Generally, you can wear most things as long as they are loose and comfortable. As you will be bending and stretching, you don't want to wear anything too restrictive. Exercise or track pants, even shorts are good, with a t-shirt or loose top.

If you do the Meridian Movements first thing in the morning, there is nothing stopping you from doing them in your nightwear, as long as you are happy to do so.

You may find that, during these Movements, you get quite thirsty, as quite a bit of heat is produced, so make sure you have a glass or bottle of water nearby. Some people also have a small towel with them, due to excess heat and sweating, which is quite common. But again, you will discover if you need this or not when you do the Movements.

When Can I Do These Movements?

The Meridian Movements can be done at any time, and it is up to you to find a time that best suits you and your lifestyle.

I usually do the Meridian Movements in the morning, as I find that if I don't, lots of other things get in the way and the day ends up slipping away.

I also find that doing the Meridian Movements in the morning allows me to get a good start on the day ahead. The deep breathing exchanges the stale, de-oxygenated blood, and replaces it with fresh, oxygenated blood. This makes me feel more awake and alive and ready to start the day in a calm, collected manner.

However, you may prefer to do them just before you go to bed, as they can relax the body and mind, allowing a peaceful sleep.

Of course, you are neither limited to doing the Meridian Movements only once a day, nor restricted to doing them only in the morning and night.

The main point is to try and get into the habit of doing the Meridian Movements on a daily basis. It may be helpful to find a regular time that you can do these Movements each day so that it becomes routine. However, everyone's lifestyle and daily demands are different, but as long as you can do them once a day, you will find it very rewarding and beneficial.

What Happens When I Do These Movements?

Before we get into the actual physical Movements, let me explain the process, in order for you to get an idea as to what is happening to your body.

Your Meridians are located in your muscles. By doing the Meridian Movements, you are gently stretching all the major muscles in your body. This stretching helps the circulation of the blood to flow more freely around the body.

Through unblocking trapped cells and eliminating deoxygenated blood, it allows fresh, oxygenated blood to take its place, and you will start to see improvement in a variety of ways.

At the beginning, you may find that some of these positions feel stiff or awkward. Even when you have been doing these exercises for a while, there may be days when some of the Movements feel more restrictive than before. I will describe ways to overcome this a bit later. This is quite common and, as long as you don't push yourself to the point of pain, it will improve.

This happens for different reasons. It can be a physical restriction which may or may not improve, depending on your individual case, whether it is an injury or surgery, etc. It can also be caused from an emotional state, due to the many stresses that occur to each of us on a daily basis.

We are not robots and our bodies are very responsive to changes in our lives, causing fluctuation on a daily basis. This usually means that the Meridians are a little stuck for now and need a bit of extra help to release the tightness. So, unless it is something major where you need medical help, there are ways to deal with it.

Alternately, when you do some of the Meridian Movements, you may find that you just want to stay in some of them. Again, this is normal and there are techniques to help with this.

I will explain in more detail in the 'How to Rebalance Your Resistant (Jitsu) Meridian for those tight areas and 'How to Rebalance Your Depleted (Kyo) Meridian sections a bit later on.

What Are The Effects?

The effects of the Meridian Movements are different for each individual, as everyone has different problems/ concerns. However, you generally should start to feel less stiffness or tension, improved mobility, calmer and less stressed.

When doing these Meridian Movements, you need to remember that we have different capabilities. Some of you will be more flexible than others, but that does not exclude you from doing the exercises, as they are adapted to suit all ages and abilities.

Keep in mind, though, that with the Meridian Movements, flexibility does not necessarily equal health.

However, you do need to know that you may experience a few unpleasant symptoms. These are caused by a build-up of toxins in your body that you have released through the Meridian Movements. You may find at the beginning that you get headaches, increased bowel Movements and/or some muscle soreness. This is perfectly normal for anyone who has never exercised before or not done any exercise for a period of time. Be kind to your body, so that each day you continue with these Meridian Movements you will find any initial symptoms lessening.

But don't worry.

These symptoms should quickly pass, so try and work through it, as each time you stop and start again you will go back to having to eliminate the build-up of toxins again.

Of course, some of you may experience no symptoms at all, but this does not mean you are doing the exercise incorrectly, so stick with it.

You will gradually start to notice that you can move more easily into each position and even start going further. This will be different for each individual, so again, as long as you do these Movements daily, you are helping yourself.

What If I Cannot Do A Meridian Movement?

Don't worry if you are finding a particular Movement too difficult to do. I will be showing alternate Movements that can be done.

This in no way affects the impact of these Movements, as it is the action and breathing that stretches the Meridians, and when done correctly you will start to feel the benefit.

What Do I Do In Each Position?

Once you have moved into the final position of each Movement, make sure your body goes back to being relaxed. As you have used your muscles to get into that position, they will have tensed, but now that you are in your position you need to physically relax the whole of your body as much as possible.

As you remain in that position, you take another deep breath in, staying relaxed, breathing out and thinking about 'letting go'.

Repeat this breath in the same position a second time, then on the next, your third breath, breathe in through the nose and into the belly; then, as you breathe out, slowly move your body back to the position you started in. Once you are back to the starting position, make sure you relax your body from the tension of moving.

Breathing Techniques

How to Breathe:

Although the principle of the breathing is very simple to do, you may find that it takes a bit of extra concentration to coordinate it with the Movements you will be doing. Be patient with yourself and soon it will become second nature.

ALL MOVEMENT IS DONE ON THE EXHALE

If you just keep this in mind throughout the Meridian Movements, then this will hold you in good stead.

Breathing – Level 1:

When you start the Movements you will be closing your eyes, but for now you can keep your eyes open and just get used to the breathing.

Practice your breathing by standing with your feet about hip width apart and knees soft (that is, not locked but comfortable).

Start by relaxing your body, especially the belly, which we all tend to try and hold in. Now relax the jaw so that the mouth is slightly open.

Staying relaxed, breathe in through your nose and feel the belly expand. When your belly has expanded as much as possible, feel the breath go into the lungs. Try not to let the shoulders rise, as this can cause tension in the neck and shoulders, which we want to avoid.

Keeping the mouth open and, maintaining your relaxed state, breathe out through your mouth. Do not push or force the exhale out, but let it flow out in a steady stream.

Remember, it is on your exhale that you will be moving into and out of each position, and your out-breath will be dictating the speed at which you do each Meridian Movement; therefore, you don't want to be breathing so rapidly that you start feeling faint, and you don't want to take so long that you lose the flow.

As mentioned earlier, it will take a bit of practice, but it will happen.

When Your Breathing Can Change

Encountering Meridian Resistance:

I mentioned earlier that, in life, we all have our ups and downs. It could be for any number of reasons, but this is life, and it rarely stays exactly the same on a day- to-day basis.

Sometimes you feel like you are this whirling dervish, trying to be everything to everybody and end up feeling stressed at the end of the day. You may have eaten something that hasn't quite agreed with you or may have had a bit too much to eat and/or drink. You may not be 'feeling yourself' or experiencing some emotional upheaval.

Whatever the reason:

THIS IS PERFECTLY NORMAL

When this happens, you will find that your body will reflect these changes. You may find that one of the Movements seems harder to perform than it did the day before.

It can also be a sign that you are pushing through unwanted blockages, releasing an area that has been restricted and stuck for some time.

It is like I previously mentioned: when you exercise for the first time or after a long break, you may experience headaches and some nausea. Do not give up as it WILL PASS.

This will probably be most noticeable when you first start practicing the Meridian Movements, due to the build-up of toxins which can cause blockages along the Meridians.

As I said, it will start to ease off after a while, but it will depend on how often you do the Meridian Movements and how blocked your Meridians are.

Even if you have been doing the Meridian Movements

for a while, you can still experience these blockages from time-to-time. Again, this is normal.

When you feel a tightness or restriction in any of the Meridian Movements, this indicates where the blockage/imbalance is, so you will need to adapt your breathing here.

Encountering Meridian Depletion:

As with all things, there are opposites, and this is true of our physical circumstances. So, if there is tightness and resistance in one area, there will be slackness and depletion somewhere else along that Meridian.

We have discussed the tightness of the physical body and how this can be caused by factors beyond our control.

This depletion is seen as an imbalance, and manifests through a feeling of emptiness along the relevant Meridian line. You may find that when you do a particular Meridian Movement, it feels like you want to stay in that position.

Just as with releasing the tight areas, by feeding this area and filling up the empty, slack area you are simultaneously helping to release the blocked, tight area in an attempt to rebalance the Meridians.

As always, with regards to any Meridian Movement that feels restrictive, so it is with any Movement that feels empty or depleted in that it indicates an imbalance and will require a different breathing technique.

Be mindful not to mistake natural suppleness for Meridian emptiness. It is a very different feeling and the more you practice the Meridian Movements the more in tune you will get with your own body.

Also, you may find that you have lots of resistance to start with and no depletion, but again, as you continue to do the Meridian Movements you will start to feel subtle variations in each of the Movements and so will need to alter your breathing accordingly.

How the Meridian Movements Allow Flow

I think of the Meridians as a long, continuous line of energy in the body. When it is working properly, there is a healthy flow all the way through. There are no obstructions or undefined boundaries, like a ball of string that unravels smoothly and easily, with no interruptions, knots or breakage.

When there is a restriction in our Movement, it can be because there is a blockage somewhere along the Meridian lines. It depends on our level of health and flexibility, but it can feel tight and a bit painful. With the string analogy, it is rather like having a knot in it. This knot restricts the  unraveling of the ball of string, or energy in the case of the Meridians. When this happens, you need to use the 'How to Rebalance Your Resistant (Jitsu) Meridian' section.

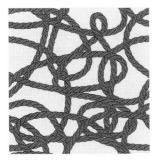

Likewise, when there is no set boundary, you can stay there, trying to work out where you are and feel equally as stuck as the Jitsu area. It is like the ball of string has lost its shape and direction and feels chaotic with no resolve in sight. When this happens you need to refer to the 'How to Rebalance Your Depleted (Kyo) Meridian' section.

How to Rebalance your Resistant (Jitsu) Meridian

When you notice that some of your Movements feel particularly stiff or you seem unable to go as far as you could the last time, or, as some of these Movements are done on one side at time, you find that one side seems to be easier than the other, use the following technique to help.

Begin by closing your eyes and relaxing your body as much as you can. Remember to check that you are not holding the belly in.

Breathe in through your nose and feel your belly expand. As you exhale through the mouth, you move your body into the stretch position, only going as far as is comfortable, but at the same time far enough to feel a bit of that tightness.

Now this is where the breathing changes. Take your next breath in as normal, through the nose, then let your breath come out your mouth quicker, like a pant or a sigh, keeping your jaw relaxed as you do so.

Repeat this breath for the next two breaths for that Movement, plus any or all of the other Movements where you feel tight or blocked.

To start with you may find you need to use this breathing technique quite often, maybe with most of the Movements. However, as you progress and do them regularly, you should find you can do the Movements more easily and thereby revert or start to use the normal breathing technique.

Please remember, though, that you may find you have to revert to the faster exhale every so often, which again is perfectly normal.

How to Rebalance your Depleted (Kyo) Meridian

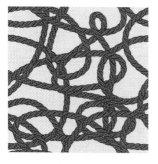

When you find yourself wanting to linger in any particular Meridian Movement, like you are too comfortable to move, you need to use the following technique.

Begin by closing your eyes and relaxing your body, making sure you are not holding in your belly. Take a slow, deep breath in, relaxing your body and letting the belly expand, then move slowly on the exhale to the Meridian Movement position.

Now pause until you feel the need to take another in breath. Slowly inhale, pause a moment, then exhale slowly. On the next, third, exhale, you move back to your original position. Repeat this two more times.

The key here is not to hurry with the Movement. Really enjoy the extended breaths, particularly when you are in the full Movement as opposed to the original position. Let yourself sink in, filling that Meridian up.

NB. I have found over the years that most people have a tendency to have particular Movements where there is tightness and another that is often empty. These are just our traits, the way our body reacts to any stressful situation. It is just who we are. It can be a headache, intestinal problems, asthma, over-eating, lack of appetite, anything.

As each Meridian Movement deals with specific organs and a specific Meridian that runs through the body, it is highly likely that, when you are stressed, it will reflect in the same Meridian Movement that it usually does.

THIS IS NORMAL.

Our bodies are just a reflection of life and as life is never the same two days running, how can our bodies be perfectly balanced all the time?

Meridian Movements can help us to keep a check on ourselves so we can prevent the body from getting too out of balance.

A Quick Recap

So, to recap, it's an OUT-BREATH to get into the position, TWO FULL BREATHS in the position, and an OUT-BREATH to get back to your original start position.

Keep in mind that the breathing is an important part of these Movements, and I will reaffirm this throughout Part Three where I describe each Meridian Movement in detail. Remember to alter your breathing when you need to, as advised previously.

The Meridian Movements are done in a specific order to allow each Movement to complement the previous one, so it's important not to skip any of the Movements. If you do skip a Meridian Movement, it interrupts the flow and can lessen the benefits. Remember that ball of string? Ignoring the knot or unraveled ball of string instead of gently correcting it only makes it worse in the long run, and you miss out on some of the benefits of the movements.

Each of these Movements has an associated Element, and so the following section goes into detail about each of the Elements and what they mean, followed by the Movement that is used to maintain balance in that Meridian.

Part Two

The Meridian Elements

Introduction

Metal   Earth   Fire   Water   Supp.Fire   Wood

In this section, you will learn about each of the six Elements that are associated with the Meridian Movements. They each have different qualities linked to them such as organs, colour, season, peak hours and personal characteristics.

The colour, season, peak hours and personal characteristics all relate to the nature of the Element, which will become clearer as you read about each one.

Where the organs are concerned, I want to explain that each Element has two organs associated with it and that each organ is linked to a Meridian line that runs through certain areas of the body. This does not mean that, if you find a Meridian Movement hard to do, there is something wrong with the associated organ, but more likely the Meridian connected to that organ. As the Meridians are located in the major muscles of the body, any tightness in a Meridian will reflect some restriction to its associated muscle.

The Metal Element

Metal

The first thought we usually have when we think of metal is something that is hard, cold and not very life-giving. So let's look beyond that and think about all the minerals found in the soil, and how these minerals provide this soil with extra richness, that then find their way into the food grown in this soil, and ultimately into our digestive system to be absorbed and utilised. Remember the saying, 'salt of the earth'? This is the very essence of the metal Element.

Metals are used as fuel for heat, strong materials for structures, and gems, such as diamonds, which have many uses from industrial drill bits to the finest surgical apparatuses – and even as a sign of love and beauty for various occasions like engagements, weddings, and anniversaries.

Think about mountain streams that flow through a network formed from metal structures from the earth. We can liken this flow and structure to the human body. We take in food, water and air to use as fuel, and eliminate what is not used, required or wanted.

Organs/Meridians

It should be no surprise that the organs associated with the Metal Element are the lungs and large intestines that deal with exchange and elimination. Lungs are used to feed the cardiovascular system by inhaling oxygen-rich air, which can then oxygenate the blood, followed by eliminating the waste product of carbon dioxide through exhalation. The large intestines are used to fuel the body by absorbing all the nutrients from our food and eliminating the waste products. These organs form the vital structure needed to maintain balance for a healthy body and mind.

Colour

The colour associated with the Element depicts its nature; for the Metal element it is silver or white, which depicts purity and clarity. It has a vitality and freshness about it with an element of stillness and calm, and a clear, creative energy about it.

Season

The season for Metal is Autumn, as this is when a lot of food is being harvested to keep us nourished through the colder months.

Peak Hours

The Elements also have specific times of the day or night allocated to them. These times are split into four consecutive hours for each Element. Within these four hours, each organ pertaining to this particular Element has its own two hours, which is why it is so important to do these Movements in a specific order and I will explain why with each Element.

The peak hours for the Lungs are between 3:00am -5:00am and, for the Large Intestine, between 5:00am - 7:00am. If we were to follow the cycle of the sun, we would be getting up early and the first thing we do when we wake up is give ourselves a good stretch and maybe a yawn or two. Both of these Movements are allowing the body to open up and take in fresh oxygen, ready for the start of a new day. Likewise, with the Large Intestine it is usually within these hours that we would defecate, having absorbed the fuel from the food we ate the night before and now needing to eliminate the waste in order to start the day fresh. These processes are referred to as exchange and elimination.

Personal Characteristics

A person who displays the following characteristics are considered to be born with Metal tendencies, but you may find that you see a bit of yourself in each of them, which is quite normal.

A person with a well-balanced Metal element likes defined boundaries and structure. They are highly organised, even meticulous, with everything clean in its place and often a list writer. They have great vitality and like to enjoy themselves, but are respectful and care about other people. They can come across as fairly reserved, but when backed into a corner, you will find that when pushed they can be very assertive and powerful.

They have an inner strength, like the ore that is mined from mountains, are self-disciplined, tenacious, self reliant and conscientious, finding it easy to study and concentrate, seeing situations very clearly, making them great problem solvers. They don't mind working or being on their own, they make wonderful observers and mediators.

If the Metal element is unbalanced, there is a tendency to be a bit impulsive, and they like to use their money to obtain luxury and power.

Because they exude and air of confidence about them, together with their determination to get things done, they can be seen as aloof; which can put a barrier up and create distance between them and their friends and co-workers.

They can have difficulty in letting go, by spending too much time in the past, or grieving for way too long, being immersed in their sadness.

They can obsess over things, going over and over something that which has already been completed. Their home is immaculate with nothing out of place. They constantly realign things to be in their exact place, even during a conversation.

They can get overly critical, be controlling, and ambitious, so any goal they have will be pursued relentlessly, with no concerns regarding obstacles or setbacks.

This can lead to them being unreasonable and stubborn at times. When they are in charge they can be quite demanding and have high expectations that others will follow their lead.

The Earth Element

Earth

When we think of earth, what immediately comes to mind? I know I think of soil, or the planet. We often refer to the 'Mother Earth', as it supplies us with our nourishment, support, and life. We walk upon it every day, and we eat foods that have been grown in it. Earth represents stability, fertility, fullness, basicness, and is the essential 'centre' of all things. The planet Earth is round, so the Element symbolises all roundness, such as circles, contours and cycles. Earth rotates on its axis, following an ovular path, and controls the cycle of life. It is said that Earth is central to all the other Elements, as everything arises from it. Metal is found in the Earth, trees from the Wood Element live above and below the Earth, Fire is at the core of the earth, and Water runs under and over the Earth. Each of the Elements has a cyclic relationship with Earth, from creation to expiration. It has been described as the never-ending cycle of life, death and rebirth.

When we talk about someone being grounded, we are referring to this person as being balanced, stable, sensible, practical, and centred. Earth people have an order and harmony within themselves, and are very 'at home' or 'at ease' with who they are. They are grounded, nurturing and compassionate. Women who display these characteristics are often referred to as 'earth mothers', as they love to feed and comfort everyone who comes to them. Their home has a very comfortable feel to it, where you know you will be well looked after and feel protected.

Organs/Meridians

The organs associated with the Earth Element are the stomach and the spleen. The stomach is where we initially receive nourishment, which is then digested and brought to fruition by passing this food energy onto the spleen for distribution. This represents us nourishing ourselves through being active and giving ourselves mental stimulation. Think of the phrase 'sick to the stomach', when we can't take something in? The spleen is seen as being in charge of the distribution and transportation of energy. In the outside world, we need this function to be able to direct information to the right place in order to act upon it. If this did not happen, then chaos would follow. As both these organs are a vital part of life: although we can live without our spleen, we are at risk of contracting serious, or life threatening infections, they are central to our healthy existence on a daily basis, you can understand why these have been associated with this Element.

Colour

The colours for the Earth Element are yellow and orange. This is said to represent the sun, ripened crops and root vegetables. When you think of these colours, images of warmth and comfort come to mind – again referring to the very core of each person.

Season

The season for the Earth Element is Late Summer, often referred to as the Indian Summer, where all the seasons seem to converge. In some references, it is said to be the last ten days of each season, referring back to it being central to all the other Elements – when everything goes back into the earth to be revitalised. By coming back to the centre and getting grounded, it allows preparation for the following season.

Peak Hours

The peak hours for the Earth Element are 7:00am - 9:00am for the stomach and 9:00am - 11:00am for the spleen. This is when the energy for the Earth is at its strongest. This is usually the time when breakfast is consumed, nourishing the body and providing fuel for the day. This is considered the most important meal of the day and one that is often overlooked. Once the food has started to be digested, the spleen then breaks down the food through digestive juices and then distributes this fuel throughout the body. It is considered to be the transporter of energy. These processes are referred to as ingestion and digestion.

Personal Characteristics

Apart from the personal characteristics described earlier, a person with a well-balanced Earth Element displays the ability to be at-home with themselves. They take good care of their needs but also feel a sense of duty to care for those close to them, without being too overbearing.

They are patient, reliable, conservative, and quite sensible with their finances. Although they are disciplined and tend not to show emotion, they still want to feel important and be loved.

Although they are ambitious, they can be unrealistic, as they are inclined to not be overly adventurous but rather enjoy their home comforts. In balance this shows up as the ability to keep things in perspective and stay grounded.

Problems are tackled in a logical, methodical manner, with the ability to use their resources prudently.

They judge the world from their moral compass, being very ethical and disciplined. They follow their intuition and use their powerful deductive talents, and together with their steadiness and reliability often impress the people around them, and are well- respected and admired.

These qualities make them ideal as carers, peacemakers, providers, planners, or administrators.

The imbalance in this Element can show up as being

someone who worries a lot. This can turn them into being overprotective, even meddlesome. Their boundaries can become unclear, leading to overworking, over-studying, or overstimulating their minds – particularly intellectually.

They can be pensive and have a fear of the unknown and, therefore, can appear to be very controlling and only interested in what they can gain for themselves.

Others can interpret this as being selfish, self-centred, stubborn, or rigid.

Physically, the Earth imbalance can show up through easily gaining weight but finding it hard to lose it again. This can lead to unclear thinking, feeling fuzzy-headed, and generally feeling stuck.

The Fire Element

Fire

When you think of fire, you think of warmth, light, active, dynamic, lively, colourful, full-of-spark, and vitality. It has an amazing presence and can be used to create and direct energy. The expression 'on fire' is used to describe someone who is full of excitement about life. Similarly, the saying 'all fired up' refers to someone who is driven by enthusiasm about something. Fire is considered a life principle, as it always refers to life in some way. As mentioned previously, it is active, it rises up, and it is alive. We refer to the qualities of fire a lot with the words: spark, flame, and ablaze—all strong, emotional representations. Think of the open fire in the home and the image of warmth; homely and love come to mind. The sun is fire; it is a life-giver, and without it all things would perish.

Organs/Meridians

As you would expect, one of the organs related to the Fire Element is the Heart, and the other the Small Intestines. The heart is the central source of life for all living creatures and is often termed the Supreme Controller, responsible for the workings of the body/mind/spirit. Like a ruler, it excels in clear insight and understanding, directing its influence for the well-being of all it rules. Physiologically, it pumps the vital oxygenated blood throughout our entire cardiovascular system, and pumps the deoxygenated blood back through the lungs to begin the cycle again, over and over. The small intestines are creating change to our fuel that has come in as food and is now being separated into what can be used (the pure energy) and what needs to be eliminated (the impure). Emotionally, it can be seen as the sorting out process, deciding what is valuable information and what is to be discarded.

Colour

The colour of the Fire Element is red. When we think of the heart, we think of red. We draw hearts to represent love and passion, and show our love for another person by giving cards with red hearts on them and red roses, especially on Valentine's Day!

Season

As you might have guessed, the season of the Fire Element is Summer. It is the time for growth, when nature blossoms and comes to fruition. Creation within all aspects of nature flourishes and grows. Life is abundant. This is true also of the body and mind. The body is not weighed down by layers of clothing, it has freedom and lightness. Living outdoors more, soaking up the sun, with lots of joy and laughter. Thoughts and ideas that were planted in the spring now flourish.

Peak Hours

The peak hours for the Fire Element are 11:00am - 1:00pm for the Heart, and 1:00pm - 3:00pm for the Small intestines. The first hours are when the food has been broken down and the Supreme Controller has decided what is going to be done with it. Physically, this relates to getting the daily duties done. The following hours use this time to carry out the order and sort the nutrients and waste products. Again, physically, this is when the order of the duties are sorted and carried out to completion, rather like an internal and external office.

Personal Characteristics

A well-balanced Fire Element can show up as someone who has tremendous charisma, with a dynamic personality who loves to socialise and talk. Combined with their decisive, brilliant, warm, and dramatic traits, they tend to create quite a magnetic attraction. They have a great capacity to love and like to create strong ties with their loved ones.

They love adventure and excitement and don't like to be hidden away from where all the action is. They enjoy competition, but can sometimes become aggressive in order to achieve their life goals, instead of being patient and compassionate.

They like exploring anything new and so have the tendency to get restless. They are the very essence of the social butterfly, with their confidence and self- assurance.

They are very calm and in-control, deep-thinking, and excellent at motivating, almost commanding people into action. They are very clever and want everyone to know this, and because they are gifted speakers they make excellent leaders.

When there is an imbalance within the Fire Element, it can bring out impatience and impulsive behaviour. This can develop into aggression, where they become selfish and inconsiderate.

Too much heat, of course, can burn instead of providing just warmth. This can lead to a person feeling burnt out, lacklustre, or bland. They can become anxious, restless, and suffer from insomnia.

The imbalance can cause the person to be overly excitable, causing them to possibly stutter, talk too much and too fast, or laugh nervously. They can be quickly stimulated to excess, or go the other way and be emotionally shut down and unfeeling.

In the work environment, they can be quite impatient when their ambition is thwarted, and when they try and force the situation in any way, they find that they come across even more frustrating obstacles, perpetuating the imbalance.

The Water Element

Water

Wet, fluid, still, raging, flowing; it takes its shape with whatever it is surrounded by. It is essential for life. Water can be hot, cold, warm, murky, or clear. We drink it and travel on it. It has force and power, ranging from a single drop to the largest ocean and everything in between. It can by rhythmic, cyclic, violent, inundating, tranquil, or submissive. It has a refreshing, invigorating quality, and we consist of about 78% of it.

Even within the body, there are ponds, rivers, seas, reservoirs, and oceans of energy. We have the flow of blood, like a river, with the veins and arteries being tributaries. The lymphatic system is another river, cleaning and clearing the blood. Then there is fluid from sweat, tears, saliva, sexual secretions, and lactation.

When someone 'goes with the flow' instead of 'swimming against the tide', their life opens up easily and effortlessly in front of them, rather than struggling with constant setbacks. The pivotal words for this Element are fluidity and flow, and can be seen as someone who is strong, fearless, and determined, who endures many hardships in pursuit of their goals, or perseveres by sheer willpower.

Organs/Meridians

The organs associated with the Water Element are the Kidneys and the Bladder. The Kidneys regulate the flow of water around the body, which is quite a task considering how much water we consist of. The flow allows waste material to be collected and disposed of through urination. The other liquid is our blood and the kidneys have just over 69 litres of blood per hour flowing through them to get purified and broken down into nutritional components.

The Bladder is in charge of eliminating the fluid waste that has been sorted by the Kidneys. It is also linked with the Kidneys' function of helping to store the Vital Essence, so the Bladder needs to be adaptable by being able to store and eliminate fluid waste, but flexible enough to hold small and large amounts of fluid without discomfort. In relation to a person, this shows as someone who is adaptable, flexible in their attitude, and comfortable with change.

Colour

The colour for the Water Element is blue. The sea is often associated with the colour blue, and is referred to in sayings such as 'the deep blue sea', or 'blue waters', in many books and poems. This, again, relates back to the natural flow of things internally and externally.

Season

Winter is the season of the Water Element. This is the time for storing energy. Many animals hibernate during the winter months. Even most of the flora stops to take a rest, and all the crops are in and the land lies fallow, restoring itself for the next season's yield. People often like to stay at home, snuggled and cozy and warm. Winter is the season with the least amount of daylight hours, so if we were to regulate our life around the natural light, we would be resting more and, therefore, conserving our energies.

Peak Hours

The peak hours for the Water Element are 3:00pm - 5:00pm for the Kidneys, and 5:00pm - 7:00pm for the Bladder. These times fall after lunch and before dinner, when the food needs to be purified and the body's fluid waste needs to be eliminated. It is said that the Water's energy is at its strongest between these hours, and a person can see their direction in life very clearly then.

Personal Characteristics

The well-balanced Water Element personalities have the ability to be very intuitive, compassionate, sensitive, and charming. Like a river or the tides, they tend to 'go with the flow', and this makes them very flexible in their thinking. Because of this, they can be very creative, with a wondrous imagination which they put to good use. This often leads them to having more than one profession, including freelancing.

They can be very good at a job that requires the use of their diplomacy, strength and willpower to get results. Through their love of a challenge and use of their adaptability, good people skills and the art of being subtly persuasive, together with the desire to seek a harmonious outcome, they make brilliant negotiators.

They use their talent for communication and intuition to find things that have eluded other people. They use their gift of noticing other people's special gifts and talents through recognition and making them feel good about their abilities. This makes them ideal for organising and delegating work to the appropriate people.

They not only make excellent philosophers and thinkers, being the Element where all great innovations and ideas are created, but they also have a flair as healers and clairvoyants.

The Water imbalance can show itself through this Element being manipulative, deceptive and secretive, and are not the type to share a secret with anyone else. This can reveal itself through anxiety, fear and, in extreme cases, phobias.

They often try to find the easiest path, like a river following the boundaries of the banks, so they have to be careful of bending too easily to the whims of others, being too reserved or passive, and not standing up for what they believe in.

The opposite imbalance to this fluid and weak state is one of great power, like a river bursting its banks or a storm. This may reveals itself through the person appearing quite eccentric.

The Supplementary Fire Element

Supplementary Fire

Although the Supplementary Fire is often tied in with the Fire Element, it does hold some different qualities. Unlike the Fire Element, which can be wild, dynamic and full of vitality, the Supplementary Fire is more associated with the steady, constant flame of a candle. It gives some warmth, but in a more subtle manner.

Organs/Meridians

The Supplementary Fire does not have specific organs as such, but it does have two specific functions. One is considered to be the pericardium, the sac that surrounds and protects the heart. This plays a vital role in controlling the flow of blood around the heart, sorting out what should and should not be allowed in and out of it, thus allowing the heart to function in a protected and unheeded fashion. Just as in life, we need that buffer zone for protecting ourselves from being attacked too deeply, mentally, emotionally, and physically in the outside world.

The other function is referred to as the Three Chou, or Triple Heater. Its overall function is to guard all the organs in the body, and control the temperature of the body. Breaking this function down further, there is the Upper Chou, located in the chest area and relating to respiration and ingestion. Here it guards the heat of the lungs and heart. Then there is the Middle Chou, located in the upper abdominal area, relating to digestion, guarding the stomach, spleen, gall bladder, liver, and small intestines. Finally, there is the Lower Chou, located in the lower abdominal area, relating to elimination and guarding the large intestines, bladder, and kidney.

Because the function of both the Heart Protector and Three Chou is to guard and protect all the other organs in the body, they are considered extremely powerful. This is also extremely important in life, making sure we stay strong and clear, preventing us from taking everything to heart and draining our resources.

Colour

The colour of the Supplementary Fire is pink because, although it is similar in many ways to the Fire Element, it is not as volatile, so it is not as vivid a colour. The colour still suggests warmth, like a glow.

Season

The Supplementary Fire Element shares the same season as the Fire Element, which is Summer, so you can refer back to this to get an idea of it.

Peak Hours

The peak hours for the Supplementary Fire Element are 7:00pm - 9:00pm for the Heart Protector, and 9:00pm - 11:00pm for the Triple Heater. The Heart Protector is often referred to as the Circulation Sex, as it is associated with making love. By following the natural rhythm of nature, we would go to bed when it gets dark, which is around this correlated time and is, therefore, considered the time for making love. This is followed by the Triple Heater, evaluating and adjusting our body temperatures so as to ensure the proper amount of heat throughout the body for a good night's sleep. Overall the main function of this Element is one of physical and emotional protection, ensuring warmth and harmony.

Personal Characteristics

The well-balanced Supplementary Fire Element is very like the balanced Fire Element, but not so extreme or volatile. So when you read about the personal characteristics of the Fire Element, you need to think of it in a gentler way.

Some of the subtle differences are that, apart from being a great protector, they have the capacity to love unconditionally. They show great kindness and have great joy and happiness.

Unlike the Fire Element, this character understands the need to allow themselves to grieve and really feel sadness when a situation calls for it. By allowing this to happen, it allows balance to be maintained.

An imbalance in this Element will not be as extreme as the Fire Element, but it can seem that these people are joyless and they seem to not be present, almost like they are invisible.

The Wood Element

Wood

Wood brings the image of a tree: strong, upright, and directional. A tree draws its energy from its roots in the earth to feed the leaves and buds. When leaves and flowers fall to the ground, they decompose, creating nourishment for the roots, whilst the seeds scatter in the wind to create new life. It is an efficient cycle of self-preservation. A tree needs to be flexible, bending and yielding to the wind, as well as strong and durable in order to survive. If a tree were unbending, it would break in a powerful storm.

The bamboo is a great example of all these qualities, as it is used in China as scaffolding, exhibiting its strength and yet, in a fierce wind it bends and sways, yet remains rooted.

This description also pertains to a person. We start as a small seed, and then get planted in this world. We have our feet firmly rooted, growing upwards and with the correct nourishment, both physically and emotionally, we become strong with a sense of direction and yet flexible enough for any changes that come about. We also carry seeds within us for new life.

Organs/Meridians

The organs of the Wood Element are the Liver and Gall Bladder. The Liver stores nutrients and energy for physical activity. It creates immunity cells to combat disease and digestive enzymes to break down fat. It detoxifies the blood to maintain physical energy and health. The role of the Liver is to continuously decide where the blood should be distributed around the body to correlate with what the person is doing.

The Gall Bladder is referred to as the decision maker. It distributes nutrients and controls the amount and balance of the numerous digestive enzymes. The Gall Bladder is considered the dispatcher, carrying out the orders of the Liver.

Relating these qualities to a person, the Liver is considered the military leader who excels in strategic planning. In everyday life, we are constantly planning, from the moment we get up with small things like what to eat and wear, to the day's tasks and even bigger things like government, laws, and even wars. The Gall Bladder is the official who is an expert in making sound decisions and judgement. Again, we are constantly making decisions related to the planning we have done, and how best to execute these plans in the most efficient manner.

Colour

The colour of the Wood Element is green. Young saplings are green, the leaves are green and, interestingly, it is the colour that we see the most shades of in our colour spectrum. In nature, particularly in Spring, when all the new shoots and saplings abound, there is an abundance of green.

Season

As mentioned above, the season for the Wood Element is Spring. This is where nature is at its greenest. Spring is the time of the saplings and shoots to push determinedly up through the earth, full of strength and vitality, clearly heading for the sun and growth. Yet, it all has to be flexible, as it may have had a stone above it beneath the soil and, therefore, will have to bend around it, or it will not survive. Spring is also the time when many creatures do their mating, sowing seeds within. People often feel fresh, vital, alive, and full of renewed energy. Ideas that have been stored over winter are often put into action to grow and develop.

Peak Hours

The peak hours of the Wood Element are 11:00pm - 1:00am for the Gall Bladder, and 1:00am - 3:00am for the

Liver . These are often the times when the day's transactions are mulled over and decisions about what to do and where to go next are made. These times correlate with the Fire Element during the day, where both these Elements deal with control and assimilation.

Personal Characteristics

The balanced characteristics of the Wood Element are people who have clear vision with specific goals. They are confident, generous, compassionate, and have a strong sense of what they consider to be ethical behaviour.

They love exploring, and like to maintain a variety of different interests. They make very loyal friends, and are not prone to self-indulgence or selfish behaviour. They deeply appreciate what they have around them or have attained without lusting after that which they feel is unreachable.

They like to be busy, with the belief that hard work does them a world of good; they are diligent and committed to their work. They really enjoy working in teams, and have excellent planning and decision skills, which can make their goals easily attainable.

They have the tendency to disagree quite forcefully and are adept at arguing their point and opinions strongly with their exceptional powers of persuasion.

You will notice them by their piercing, penetrating eyes, and they make great leaders, pioneers, and strategists because of their amazing foresight. They are considered artists in whatever profession, or professions, they choose.

A Wood imbalance can be seen as someone who is indecisive, lacking direction in life, or seemingly stuck. They can be arrogant, angry, and overly controlling, taking on more than they can handle, becoming overwhelmed due to them not accepting their limits. This imbalance can cause an addictive personality, becoming workaholics and, possibly, drug and alcohol abusers. This can develop into an overdependence on others.

Part Three

The Meridian Movements

Before You Start

Just remember, the Meridian Movements are meant to be slow and gentle, and although it may seem a lot to take in at first, just like learning anything for the first time, it wasn't accomplished overnight, so take your time and enjoy the experience.

Just a reminder that these six simple Meridian Movements are done in the order they are described below to get the most out of them. There are alternative Movements included for those of you who might find some of them a bit hard to start with. So just play around with them to what suits you, and enjoy.

Metal

1. Metal Meridian Movement

Stand comfortably, with your feet a hip width apart and your toes facing inwards.

Put your arms behind you, linking your thumbs together, letting your hands rest on your body. It does not matter which way you link your thumbs; place them however is more comfortable for you.

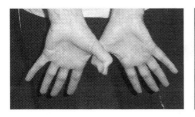 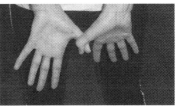

Keeping as relaxed as you can, breathe in, feeling your belly expand. As you breathe out, lift your linked hands up behind you, as far as is comfortable for you, then, with your knees bent slightly, start to bend your upper body forward, again as far as is comfortable. Now straighten your legs and keep them straight throughout this Movement.

This Movement is all done on the exhale. Don't worry if it takes a little longer to begin with, you will soon get used to what you need to do and find it easier to remember.

In that bent position, you need to make sure you remain as relaxed as possible.

Take another deep breath in, feeling the belly expand first as you fill your lungs. On the exhale, you may feel yourself going a little further, but please don't worry if it doesn't happen.

Repeat this breath, remaining in this position, feeling as if you are letting go of any tension you feel. The main thing is to stay relaxed.

Now, breathe in again, and on your exhale you are going to slowly bring your body to the upright position. Try to feel like your arms are gently pulling you upright, but keep your head lowered toward your chest, otherwise you might strain it. Your arms and head are the last things to return to the starting position.

After each Movement, always remember to check that you are relaxed, because, as mentioned earlier, you have used your muscles to move and now you need to release any tension.

Great! Now, this Movement is repeated another two times. Just remember to stay relaxed, don't rush, and always move on the exhale.

You should feel a stretch along your arms, across the chest, and down the backs of your legs. If you are not used to any stretching, you could feel it in more places, but be gentle with yourself and make sure you do not overstretch, as this will do more harm than good.

1a. Metal Meridian Complementary Movement

There is a complementary Movement, which you can start with if you find the basic Movement a little difficult to begin with. You can try alternating between the basic and complementary with all the Movements.

Stand on one foot with your knee slightly bent. Put the other foot behind with your toes touching the floor. It looks like you have taken a step forward. Raise your arms to where they are comfortable.

As you exhale, lift yourself up onto the front foot and lift your heel off the floor. At the same time, stretch your arms up and out, almost as if you are flying. Repeat this about ten times, five on each foot. Please note that your breathing may be a little faster, which is fine.

Earth

2. Earth Meridian Movement

This Movement is started on the floor, in a kneeling position. Think about kneeling up then sitting back down. If possible, have your feet either tucked under your bottom or to the side of your thighs. If this is too hard to do yet, stay kneeling up or look at the complementary Movements.

As you exhale, lower your body onto the

mat, using your elbows to help you down. Your knees will probably lift up off the mat, which is fine. Now raise your arms above your head, linking your hands with the palms facing toward the head.

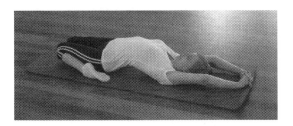

Stay in that position, breathing in deeply through the nose, feeling your belly expand, then breathing out. After repeating this another two times, bring yourself back up, on the exhale, again using your elbows and hands, to the kneeling position. Then, bend forward over your knees to release the body for a breath. Come back to the kneeling position and repeat this Movement twice more.

You should feel a stretch along the front of the legs and torso and along the arms.

As this Movement can be difficult for some, I suggest that you try these alternatives to find which one suits you to begin with and slowly progress towards the one shown here. However, if you are unable to ever get to this position that is fine, just as long as you don't skip this Movement.

2a. Earth Meridian Complementary Movement - 1

This Movement starts with kneeling up then putting your hands on the mat behind you and, on the exhale, pushing your hips forward until you feel a gentle stretch.

Stay in this position for two full breaths, then come up to kneeling on the third exhale. Repeat this twice more.

When this Movement becomes easier, you may want to alternate between this and the basic one, by gently easing your body back, on the exhale, until you are on your elbows. If you find that you have enough of a stretch leaning back on your elbows, then stay there, using your arms to support you. If you can tilt your head back a bit, it helps, but don't overextend the neck. If and when you feel ready you can start doing the basic Movement.

The whole Element Movement is repeated three times, whether you are alternating between the Movements or not.

2b. Earth Meridian Complementary Movement - 2

Another complementary Movement is sitting on your feet with knees apart in a 'v' shape. As you exhale, use the same hand as the knee to bring the knee up towards you and, at the same time, lean your body slightly forward to meet the knee, then repeat with the other side. Your breathing will be quite a bit faster with this one so please don't worry. You may find that one leg is easier than the other, so just go a bit higher with that leg and try not to force the other leg to go any higher than is comfortable. You can repeat this Movement between 10 to 14 times. You can try alternating between this Movement and any of the previous ones to see if there is improvement.

NB. This is a great Movement to help digest food quicker.

2c. Earth Meridian Complimentary Movement - 3

Finally, if kneeling is not an option for this Movement, then you can stand up against a wall. Put your hand on the wall as high as it will go and then hold the outside leg with your other hand. If this is not possible, you could just bend the knee or use a chair to place your knee on.

As you exhale, stretch the body by pulling the bent leg backwards and stretching the arms up as far as they will comfortably go. Repeat this three times on each leg.

This Movement can be a challenge, and if you find this to be so, then here is where you will use the quick breathing technique. Stay for the three breaths, moving in and out of the Movement on the exhale, repeating it three times. You will surprise yourself as to how much easier this will get after a while.

Fire

3. Fire Meridian Movement

The fire Meridian Movement begins in a seated position, with legs in front, knees bent and the soles of the feet touching, as shown. Bring your feet as near to your body as you can. Your hands are holding your feet.

Get relaxed, breathe in deeply, expanding the belly. Watch for any shoulder tension. On the exhale, lower your body forward, keeping hold of your feet and making sure the arms and elbows stay in front of your legs, not tucked into the body. Stay in this position for your three breaths, and then, on the third exhale, bring yourself back to the sitting position. Check your shoulders each time to make sure they remain relaxed. Repeat another two times.

If your feet don't touch, just bring them in as far as is comfortable. Likewise, if you cannot reach your feet, put your hands on your legs as close to your feet as they will go. When you move into the second position on your exhale, make sure your elbows are away from your body.

You should feel a stretch on the insides of your legs and along the inside and under arm. You may also feel a stretch along your back and in your hips, which is fine.

3a. Fire Meridian Complementary Movement

The complementary Movement to the Fire Element starts in basically the same way: by sitting on the floor, bringing your feet together and as close to your body as is comfortable. Lean forward to hold the toes, or, if not possible, as far down the leg as is possible.

With the elbows pointing outward as far as possible, gently rock your body on an exhale to one side, breathing in as you return to the centre and then rocking to the other side on another exhale, again returning to the centre. Repeat this Movement for about five or six  times and then, if you want, try the basic Movement again. As with all the Movements, you can alternate between the basic and complementary, as long as you complete the whole Movement three times.

Water

4. Water Meridian Movement

The starting position for the Water Meridian Movement is sitting with your legs out in front of you. Keep your legs a hip-width apart, so they are running parallel. Have your feet pointing upwards, in a flexed position. You may already be able to feel a stretch along the back of the legs, which is fine. Raise your arms straight up in the air, to either side of your head. Have the palms of your hands facing toward each other.

Relax your shoulders and take a deep breath in. As you exhale, lower your body, keeping the arms by your head as you go down, until your arms are parallel with your legs. Keep your feet flexed, and don't lower the arms. Stay there for your three breaths, coming back to sitting up on the third exhale.  Check that your shoulders have not tensed, then repeat twice more.

To begin with you may find you can't get parallel with your legs, so just go as far as you can, making sure you feel a comfortable stretch, not a painful stretch, as that will tense the body up and defeat the purpose. Keep your arms by your head. If you need to lower your arms between each set, that's fine, just make sure they don't tense up during the Movement.

You should feel a stretch down the back, along the arms and the back of your legs.

4a. Water Meridian Complimentary Movement

The complementary Movement starts in the same position as the basic one, but instead of lowering the body, you walk on your bottom, moving forward and backward with your arms following your legs. Make sure you keep your feet flexed and the palms facing toward each other. Have the same arm stretched forward as the leg you are moving forward, then move the other leg and arm in the same manner. Exhale with each move forward. Your breathing may be slightly quicker which is fine. Walk forward for four and back for four, three times in all. As always, you can alternate between the complementary and basic Movements.

Supplementary Fire

5. Supplementary Fire Meridian Movement

This Movement starts in the sitting position, with legs crossed. The left leg goes nearest to your body to begin with. Now cross your arms over in front of you, with the left arm nearest your body. Your palms need to face upwards and as close to the top of your legs as possible.

Relax and take a deep breath in and, as you exhale, lower your upper body to as far as it will comfortably go. Let the head relax, chin to chest, so there is no tension in the neck. Stay there for two full breaths and, on the third exhale, slowly come back to the starting position.

After doing this Movement for three times, swap over the leg and arm, so that the right leg and arm is nearest to your body, and repeat the whole Movement sequence from the beginning. That is to say, three breaths three times.

Don't worry if you can't get your legs or arms close to your body; as long as you follow the sequence of left leg and arm, then the right leg and arm, you are doing it correctly.

You should feel a stretch across the upper back and along the arms and down the sides of the legs.

5a. Supplementary Fire Complimentary Meridian Movement

The complementary movement for this element is aptly named a bear hug as you literally hug yourself. Stand with your legs a little wider than your shoulder width. Wrap your arms around yourself so that you are hugging your shoulders. Try both ways to find out which one is more comfortable and stay with that one. The upper body needs to be tilted forward and you will twist your body to the opposite side of whichever arm is on top, i.e. if your left arm is on top, you turn to the right, stretching all down the left side first.

So, whilst grasping your shoulders and as you exhale, tilt your upper body slightly forward and twist round as far as you can go to the point where the heel of the opposite leg comes off the floor, but keep pushing down on that heel for a better stretch.

Now inhale as you return to the starting position then exhale and continue to gently swing to the other side, in one smooth movement. You may notice it is more restricted, which is perfectly normal. Continue to swing from side to side for about five stretches each side. Again your breathing will be slightly faster which is fine.

Wood

6. Wood Meridian Movement

The Wood Meridian Movement starts by sitting up, but this time you have one leg bent at the knee, tucked in to the body, with the other leg straight and as far out to the side as it will comfortably go, keeping this foot flexed. Before you start, try this position with the right and left foot tucked and the opposite leg stretched out and, whichever side is easier, start on that side.

Raise your arms above your head, palms facing each other, keeping your shoulders relaxed.

Take a deep breath in and, as you exhale, lower your upper body to the side of the outstretched leg, without twisting, as far as is comfortable. You should still be facing forward—looking out, not towards your leg. In this position, using the hand nearest the foot, try and hold the big toe with your thumb. Both palms should now be facing upwards. The upper hand needs to turn so that the palm is also facing upward. Take your deep breaths in this position, relaxing as much as possible, and come back to sitting upright on the third exhale.

When you have completed the three cycles on this side, swap over to the other side and repeat the Movements.

This Movement can be quite a challenge to a lot of people, so again, like the Earth Meridian Movement, do quicker breaths. Remember to only go into the Movement until you feel a comfortable stretch, or you will create tension in your body and could hurt yourself. If your leg cannot tuck right into your body, that is fine—just get it as close as you can. The same goes for the side-bend, as you don't want to cause so much tension that you cannot find a point of relaxing the muscles.

If you need to lower your arms between each Movement, that is also fine, just keep those shoulders relaxed.

You should feel a stretch on the insides of your legs, down the side of your body and along the arms. You may also feel a stretch in your bottom and hips.

6a.Wood Meridian Complimentary Movement

The complementary Wood Element Movement starts in the same position as the basic Movement. Again, go on the side that is easiest first. As you exhale, twist your body round to the side of your bent knee, using your hands to help support you. Look back over your shoulder and you should feel a stretch all through your body. Repeat this Movement three times on each side.

Additional Movements

Roll and Twist – For the back and neck

I have included these extra Movements, as they can really help the back and neck to get a good stretch and release any hidden, built up tension. Being a dancer meant my body was often going into some very odd positions and sometimes I felt like my back was a tight concertina. By doing this stretch, followed by a gentle twisting, it helped unknot my spine and neck, thus helping prevent the possibility of an injury.

Please note that when I first tried the roll, I could not stay in that position AT ALL. I would roll and flop right back. That is normal, as our backs are not used to this type of stretching. I suggest that you, like I did, roll back and forth at least five times, getting your body used to this Movement and slowly opening up the spine. You may get to the point where you can use your arms to hold yourself in the position and eventually be able to go the whole way, with your arms above your head. If you are not able to do this for any reason, that is okay, as long as you are able to rock a bit. You can also try holding your knees and rocking. The idea is to gently curl and stretch your spine, so please don't worry if you can't do this as the picture shows.

Roll

Start by sitting up with your knees bent in towards you and your arms by your side. As you exhale, roll backwards with the aim of getting your legs over your head. Remain in this position for 5 full breathes. You can use your arms to hold you there as long as you are not straining to stay in the position. If you are, let your body roll back and repeat five times.

With the last exhale, let your body roll back until you are in the position you started in, with your legs bent in, then let your body naturally lay down, with your arms and legs flopping down.

Twist

Staying in the position of lying on your back, arms out at a 90-degree angle to the body, bend one knee up towards yourself and then let it roll over the other leg to the opposite side, keeping your arms outstretched and your other leg as straight as possible without forcing it. Try and keep your head turned away from the direction of the bent leg.

As you exhale, gently rock your bent leg back and forth in that position and, at the same time, slowly bring your knee up towards your shoulder as far as it will go and then down towards the other leg as far, if it will.

When you need to inhale, just pause your Movement until you are ready to exhale again.

Quick Guide

To help you when you are first starting out, I have a free bonus online 'Quick Guide' so you can see at-a-glance each Meridian Movement in the order they are meant to be done. Just go to my website to download your free copy at releaseyourstress.com.au, or email me at penny@releaseyourstress.com.au. Although this will show the basic Movement only, you can continue to use whichever Movement suits you, as long as they are done in the correct order.

At first, you will probably have to play around with which Movement suits you best at this time and start from there.

To do this, I recommend you try the basic set of each Movement, then if you need to, go to the complimentary sets of that Movement. Do each one in the same manner.

Just remember not to double-up any of the exercises. Also, if you are starting with any or all of the alternative Movements, check your ability with the first set of Movements every so often.

It is okay if you still need to remain with the complimentary exercises; however, you may be surprised at the outcome.

By using the quick guide, you are able to flow more easily from one Movement to the next instead of having to constantly stop and refer to your book.

The reason behind this is because, when you get familiar with the Meridian Movements and no longer need to refer to the quick guide, you are able to focus more on your breathing and relaxing so you get even more out of them.

Lastly though, these are meant to be an enjoyable experience so that after you do them, you can feel focused, relaxed and calm, knowing your mind and body are improving every day.

Blessings,

Penny Cooper

Printed in the United States
By Bookmasters